TREASURE CHESTS™

ANCIENT CHINA

2,000 YEARS OF MYSTERY AND ADVENTURE TO UNLOCK AND DISCOVER

D1714960

CONTENTS

CHAO-HUI JENNY LIU

WHAT'S IN THE TREASURE CHEST?

Your treasure chest is packed full of amazing items! There is a Chinese calligraphy set; a Chinese fan for you to decorate; a board and pieces to play Chinese chess; a Chinese calendar disk; a chart with Chinese gods and goddesses; a model of a watchtower from the Great Wall for you to assemble; and I Ching coins to use.

The Fan
In your tray you will find a Chinese-style fan. You can decorate this, just as the ancient Chinese used to do. Match the stickers in your secret drawer with the dotted outlines on the fan.

I Ching Coins
In your tray there are three I Ching coins. I Ching is an ancient Chinese system of fortune-telling, combining the wisdom of Taoism and Confucianism. In your secret drawer there is an instruction sheet which teaches you how to use the coins.

The Watchtower
In the secret drawer is a model of a Great Wall watchtower for you to make, an instruction sheet that shows you how to assemble the pieces, and stand-up guards and warriors to place around the finished tower.

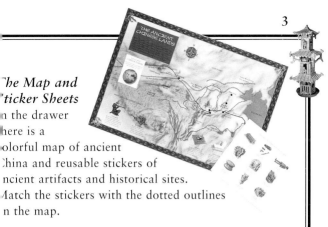

The Map and Sticker Sheets

In the drawer there is a colorful map of ancient China and reusable stickers of ancient artifacts and historical sites. Match the stickers with the dotted outlines on the map.

The Gods Chart

On the reverse side of the map is an illustrated chart of some of the most important gods and goddesses worshipped in ancient China.

Chinese Brush and Ink Set

In the tray there is a bamboo-handled calligraphy brush, an ink stick, and an ink stone for grinding the ink stick to make ink. There is an instruction and practice sheet in your secret drawer so you can try writing just like the scholars of ancient China.

Calendar Disk

In the drawer is a calendar disk which you can use to tell your horoscope according to the Chinese year. Look at the instuction sheet in your drawer to see how.

Chinese Chess

In your drawer there is a board and pieces, with an instruction sheet that shows you how to play this game of strategy.

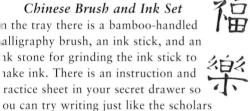

THE LAND OF CHINA

*China is part of the huge continent of Asia.
It has a variety of landscapes including deserts,*

*high mountain ranges, and fertile
river valleys. The land resembles
three steps in a staircase, going
down from west to east. The
highest step is the Tibetan Plateau,
where China's two main rivers
begin. The second step includes the
Sichuan Basin. The third step
consists of low hills and plains.*

The two main rivers in China are the
Changjiang (3,915 miles long) and
the Huang He (3,011 miles long). Both flow from the
west into the eastern China Sea. The Chinese have
used these two rivers for thousands of years to irrigate their rice fields, called paddies, and for transporting goods and people from one end of the empire to the other. The Huang He River is also called the Yellow River because it is the muddiest river in the world and can carry more than half ton of dirt per cubic yard of water! As a result, its banks are replete with rich soil. However, these rivers

*The Changjiang River, also called
the Long River, flows across
southern China. Fleets of merchant
ships once carried rice, tea, salt,
and silk along this river, from one
end of the empire to the other.*

have not always proved useful to the Chinese. The
Huang He is also known as China's Sorrow because it
often floods during the rainy season, sometimes
burying whole villages under a layer of mud.

This painting, entitled The Journey of Minhuang to Shu, *depicts the mountainous landscape of western China.*

A Broad and Diverse Land

Ancient China covered 1,800,000 square miles – about half the size of modern China. The land was comprised of hills, alluvial plains, and river valleys. The area was almost entirely surrounded by high mountains, including Mount Everest in the southwest, the highest mountain in the world. The Siberian steppes (grassland) lie in the northeast, while the great Gobi Desert stretches towards the northwest.

Inside your secret drawer, there is a map of ancient China, with reusable stickers of sites and artifacts that can be found there.

Flora and Fauna

China has a wide variety of animals and plants: 30,000 species of seed plants and 2,500 species of forest trees. Many plants were important economically. Star anise was used as a food flavoring, and sap from lacquer trees was used to glaze wooden items such as bowls and cups. Rare animals, such as the great paddlefish of the Changjiang, and small alligators in central and eastern China, can only be found here.

In the wild, giant pandas are only found in the cold mountain areas of Tibet and Sichuan.

In China, farmers cut terraces, or steps, into the hillsides in order to create more land for farming.

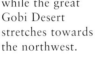

WHO WERE THE ANCIENT CHINESE?

The people of ancient China called themselves the people of Hua. Their land was central Hua. They probably looked Mongolian, as the Chinese do today.

This man has typical Mongoloid features – tan skin and dark, slightly slanted eyes.

The earliest human Chinese people are thought to have lived near present-day Beijing more than 12,000 years ago. Between 7000 and 2000 BC, Neolithic (late Stone Age) peoples lived all along the fertile Huang He River basin and on the eastern coast. These people were the first farmers, hunters, herders, and pottery and jade craftworkers in China.

The figure above formed the knob and lid of a Neolithic ceramic container. It is one of the earliest prehistoric images of a human being.

2000 BC–AD 220

Like their Neolithic ancestors, the Shang people (see page 8) were also farmers and herders. However, they were renowned for their skillful bronze metalwork. Shang rulers built walled towns and cities from which they ruled the mainly rural population. Around 1000 BC, the Shang were overrun by the warlike Zhou peoples from western China. As the Zhou empire grew,

This is the face of a terra cotta warrior. An army of these was discovered in the tomb of the First Emperor (see page 32).

it became a mixing ground for people of different races. Fierce tribes from the north raided and perhaps intermarried with the Hua. During the Han dynasty (207 BC–AD 220), the empire grew out of the Huang He region towards the south, making contact with the Man people of southeastern China.

Barbarians

After the fall of the Han, northern China was overrun by people from the north whom the Chinese considered to be less civilized than themselves. As a result, the Chinese called them barbarians. Many barbarian leaders were devout Buddhists (see pages 18–19). They set up small states in northern China and built huge stone caverns filled with carvings of Buddhist gods that can still be admired today in Luoyang.

This Tang dynasty figure shows a slave boy. He has dark skin and curly hair. The figure is early evidence that the Chinese kept foreign slaves.

This Neolithic bowl, found in the Huang He region, was placed in a tomb to indicate the wealth of the occupant.

People from Abroad

Foreign peoples have always lived in China. Travelers, such as Arabian traders, Indian monks, and Sogdian (central Asian) merchants settled in major religious and trade centers in China. They established small communities which still maintain a separate way of life from the Chinese.

The musicians shown riding this Bactrian (two-humped) camel were northern peoples, indicated by the pointed, full beards.

8

FOUR HISTORICAL PERIODS

Throughout most of its history, China has been ruled by a succession of dynasties (ruling families). This is known as the "dynastic cycle."

This painting shows Prince Zheng, the First Emperor of China

China's first great dynasty was the Shang. Its rulers were priest-kings, thought to possess the power to communicate with their royal ancestors. They used oracle bones made from ox shoulder or tortoise shells, and carved questions on them. They then scorched the bones in fire, and interpreted the cracks as answers from the spirits. Chinese writing is thought to have begun during the Shang dynasty.

The Zhou Dynasty

During the Zhou dynasty, land was divided by the ruling king into smaller states governed by *zhu hou* or lords. Eventually, the king began to lose control of these lords, and a time of conflict followed called the Warring States period. Competing lords often captured the children of their *zhu hou* enemies and

During the Warring States period, each kingdom issued its own money in shapes like these knife-shaped bronze coins.

Timeline

SHANG c.1650–1027 BC	ZHOU 1027–256 BC	WARRING STATES PERIOD 403–221 BC	QIN 221–207 BC
The Shang was China's first great dynasty. Shang rulers possessed the first written Chinese language.	Society was organized on a feudal system. Lords ruled the peasants from large estates.	With the decline of the Zhou, lords fought each other for supremacy.	Prince Zheng conquered all of China, creating the fir Chinese empire in 221 BC.

used them as hostages. Prince Zheng was once such a hostage. In 221 BC he conquered all of China, uniting it under the Qin dynasty. He became the First Emperor of China (221–207 BC).

The Shang dynasty was well-known for its metalwork, such as this bronze cooking vessel.

The Han Dynasty

After Zheng's death, Liu Bang, a minor Qin official, led a peasant army that overthrew the Qin dynasty, and he became the first emperor of the Han dynasty. This lasted for 400 years as a mighty military empire. Liu Bang started the civil service that was to rule China for the next 2,000 years.

The Period of Disunity

Wu Zetian (AD 624–705) was the only woman to rule China. She had the title of emperor.

After the fall of the Han, China entered the Period of Disunity. Northern China was divided into several kingdoms, ruled by northern barbarians. In the south, power was dominated by Han noble families.

The Sui and the Golden Tang

In AD 581, China was reunited under the Sui dynasty. But 37 years later, it was usurped by the Tang dynasty. The Tang was a prosperous period in which trade and art flourished. It is referred to as China's golden period.

HAN BC–AD 220	PERIOD OF DISUNITY 221–581	SUI 581–618	TANG 618–906
generals led s against uns in the ern steppes, ing lands as Vietnam.	China divided into a number of barbarian states. Buddhism grew in popularity.	The Sui dynasty lasted only 37 years, but reunited northern and southern China.	The Tang was a blend of Han and foreign influences. China became a great power. A golden period.

FAMILY LIFE

The Chinese character for family, or jia (shown right), represents a pig sheltered by a roof. This is symbolic because the pig usually represents wealth. A Chinese home consisted not only of a mother and father, but also all the sons and their wives and children, and any unmarried daughters, for as many generations as possible.

家

When a family member died, their name was carved onto a wooden plaque and placed on the family altar. The most senior man in the family led the others in burning incense, offering food and wine, as well as paying respects (by bowing) at the altar. It was believed that this would make the ancestor happy and that he or she would watch out for the family and its fortunes. Ancestors were honored during the annual festival of Qingming, when relatives visited their ancestors' tombs and left offerings of food and paper money.

In this painting, a family i shown giving thanks to th gods for a good harvest an plentiful rain.

Mothers and Daughters

Women had little influence or power in Chinese society. Girls were taught to obey the three men in their lives: the father in childhood, the husband when she married, and her son in old age. Widows were expected to remain

This picture was used to instruct ladies on correct court behavior, which included never addressing their lord by name.

Even today, nomadic families on the northern steppes live in yurts (movable tents), as their ancestors did centuries ago.

faithful to their dead husbands. Daughters often had their marriages arranged for them. In rural areas, some families were so poor that they would give away their daughters as child brides to be raised in the household of her husband. The bride, not much older than 10 or 12, would often babysit her 5-year-old husband! During the Tang dynasty (AD 618–906), women gained more freedom. They were allowed to remarry and noble women were even encouraged to ride horses, wearing a thin veil over their faces and short-sleeved blouses.

The Duties of Children

Chinese children were taught to respect and obey their parents. As part of their morning duties, the older children had to rise early, beat out their blankets, fold them, sweep the courtyard and floors, and prepare breakfast for their parents.

This 12th-century painting shows a son and his wife paying their respects to his parents. The respect owed by a child to his parents was called filial piety.

A large Chinese family lived in separate buildings around a square courtyard.

Women and children did household chores and worked in the rice fields.

GOVERNMENT AND SOCIETY

The first Chinese rulers were priest-kings who people believed could speak to spirits. Later, emperors were regarded as the Sons of Heaven and had absolute control over their empire. However, Chines rulers left the everyday affairs to civil servants, who were selected from the educated classes by examinations.

onfucius (551–479 BC) was the most famous sage (or wise man) in China. He was born during the Warring States period, and was still baby when his father, a famous warrior, died. So Confucius was raised by his mother, who made sure he learned the gentlemanly arts of poetry, prose, rituals music, archery, charioteering, and mathematics. He taught these arts to anyone, rich or poor, and said that a man should be judged by his behavior, rather than his backgroun and class. Confucius believed in a gentle society, where the emperor was just and the family was strong

Confucius believed that strong family relationships were important. He encouraged people to worship their ancestors.

Graduate civil servants secured some of the most prestigious jobs in Chinese society. They had many duties, which included enforcing law and order, as shown in the painting below.

The First Emperor ruled his subjects harshly. When his scholars criticized him, as shown in the painting above, he burned their books and executed anyone who disagreed with him.

Examinations

In 124 BC, the Han emperor Wu Di founded the imperial university and introduced the civil service examinations. All men could take the examinations, which were based upon a deep knowledge of the Confucian classics (see pages 28–29), and win a high position in government. The top three scorers in one year would often be summoned to the palace for a special banquet with the emperor. Sometimes, the emperor would offer such a man a princess as his bride. But for every student who passed, hundreds more failed. Students suffered days of testing in an individual hut about half the size of a telephone booth, with only food, water, ink brush, and papers. This process was just one part of what was known as China's "examination hell."

The Palace and the City of Officials

The emperor's palace was divided into two distinct areas – the private rooms of the emperor in the northern part and the government buildings to the south. Most civil service departments, such as waterways and canals, the treasury, the emperor's secretaries, and the imperial university, operated from this complex. They kept in touch with the rest of China using courier systems of horses, boats, and foot runners.

This figure shows a civil servant. These people worked in government buildings south of the emperor's own private apartments.

LIFE ON THE LAND

Most people in ancient China lived and worked in the countryside. The staple crop in the warm climate of the south was rice. The drier, slightly colder climate around the Huang He river basin was more suited to growing millet, which could be ground into a coarse flour.

Farmers originally had to do everything by hand – breaking the earth with a wooden hand plow, hoeing, and planting each young rice plant individually in the soft mud. During a drought, farmers had to carry water to their fields, one bucket at a time. During the Han dynasty (207 BC–AD 220) more efficient methods were developed.

The Grand Canal stretched for more than 600 miles. It connected the valleys of the Huang He and Changjiang rivers, so that food could be sent from the south to the imperial capitals in the north.

Watering the Land
New irrigation machines brought water from ditches and streams into the rice fields, called paddies. The most widely used of these machines needed two

This Chinese ink rubbing shows scenes from everyday life in the fertile region of Sichuan

laborers to turn the foot pedals of a large cogwheel. This pulled up a chain of wooden pallets, along which water flowed into the paddies. From AD 204, rice farmers used a "burn and drown" method for weeding. Basically, the weeds were burned.

This earthenware sheep pen dates from the Han dynasty. As well as growing rice, farmers also kept sheep, horses, and oxen.

Then, when the new weed shoots and rice grew to about 5 inches tall, the farmers cut down all the weeds and brought in water – drowning the weeds while the rice heads, well above the water, prospered.

Peasant Life

Life in the countryside was hard. Although most farmers worked on their own farms, they had to pay government taxes, serve in the army, and work for a number of days a year on public works, such as the Great Wall, canals, and roads. Women wove, cooked, and cleaned the house, as well as worked alongside the men in the fields. Older children took care of the younger ones, and brought food and water to the workers in the paddies. The harvested grain was then brought back to the house. Most Chinese houses had a courtyard, and in peasant homes this was used as a working space. The grain was threshed and dried on straw mats. Food stores were built on stilts to protect them from the rats and dampness.

At harvest time, everyone in the family worked hard in the rice fields, as the painting above shows.

In an early spring ritual, farmers carried a clay bull into the fields and then whipped it to pieces. They believed that the life-force of the bull sank into the ground, driving away the cold weather.

CITIES IN ANCIENT CHINA

The earliest Chinese cities were forts built by Neolithic people to protect their harvests. Years later, the Shang kings built walled cities which were centers for bronze, bone, and pottery workshops. As subsequent empires grew, some cities became the capitals of dynasties.

F rom around AD 589, Chinese towns and cities were built on a grid system in the shape of a square, symbolizing the four corners of the world. In dynastic capitals, one main boulevard passed through the city from north to south, ending at the gates of the imperial palace. Each city was divided into walled sections, called wards, which were locked each evening. A warning would sound from a central tower

This painting depict Kaifeng, an important 12th century merchant city. I shows the hurly-burly of cit life and evokes the flavor o ancient Chang'an

when the gates to the ward were about to close Inside, university students engaged in the city's nigh life. They sat in the tea houses and inns until all hours of the morning – drinking, singing, and composing poetry until the gates reopened and they could go home.

The painting on the left is of the Forbidden City, where the emperor resided. Built in the 15th century, it was similar to the imperial palaces of the Tang dynasty.

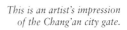

The City of Chang'an

Chang'an may have been the greatest city in China. By the time of the Han dynasty (207 BC–AD 220), it was the

This is an artist's impression of the Chang'an city gate.

capital of the Chinese empire and boasted a population of a quarter million. During the Tang dynasty (AD 618–906), Chang'an doubled in size. The rich lived in the east end of the city, and the poor in the west because the latter area tended to flood during the rainy season. Rich families lived in houses with many stories, built with cross-beams and rafters covered with ornate carvings. The houses were furnished with sculptures, paintings, and expensive draperies. The imperial palace had many towers, surrounded by pleasure gardens stocked with exotic animals and plants.

Markets

Markets were usually situated along the main avenues of the city. They were used as meeting places for travelers from all parts of Asia. People sold anything from noodles to grape wine, camels, horses, and even slaves. Market squares were also the site of public executions. Stealing a horse was once considered a capital offence.

This is a pottery model of a central tower dating from the Han dynasty.

TAOISM AND BUDDHISM

Chinese religious beliefs were known as the "three ways": Buddhism (from India), Taoism (home grown), and Confucianism (see pages 12–13). Most Chinese people practiced a combination of these three religions.

Laozi, pictured above, was said to have been an imperial librarian.

Laozi was the mythical founder of Taoism. In one story, Laozi disappeared to the west on a green ox, but before passing out of China, wrote down his wisdom in a scroll and left it with a gatekeeper. This is why he is usually depicted as an old man with a scroll or sitting on an ox (as pictured above left). Taoists believed people should live simply and in harmony with nature. For this reason, Taoism became very popular during the Warring States period (403–221 BC), when there was constant political turmoil. Taoism also promoted alchemy (a form of chemistry) and magical practices. Taoist priests mixed together different substances, in the hope of discovering an elixir of life that would make them immortal.

Buddhism

Buddha (born *c.* 563 BC) was a north Indian prince. He gave up his wealth and power in order to find

Find out more about Chinese gods and goddesses by looking at the chart inside your secret drawer.

personal peace and enlightenment. Buddha, whose name means Enlightened One, taught that by giving up worldly desires, such as fine horses or good food, one would be released from the sorrows of the world and reach a blissful state, called Nirvana.

Although the Chinese resisted Buddhism at first, the Buddhists found champions in the rulers of the small northern kingdoms in China during the Period of Disunity (AD 221–581).

This stone head is of a Bodhisattva, or "enlightened being." They were a kind of Buddhist deity.

The Afterlife

Chinese people worshiped their ancestors and believed that the spirit world was similar to the real one. They prepared their loved ones for the afterlife by placing objects in their graves. Clay models of houses, sheep and pig pens, granaries, horses and oxen were put inside their tombs. Relatives also decorated the tombs with murals of banquets, acrobats, musicians, guardian spirits, beautiful women, and servants. Sometimes real banquets were laid out in the tombs.

Earthenware figure of a tomb guardian from the Tang dynasty (AD 618–906). Relatives placed pottery figures such as this in the tombs of their loved ones.

The tombs of Chinese rulers often contained beautiful objects. This jade shroud belonged to Liu Sheng of the Han dynasty (207 BC–AD 220). The Chinese believed that jade, a hard stone, had magical properties that helped preserve the body after death.

THE SILK ROAD

The Silk Road was the name given to a series of routes that ran from northern China across Asia. Chinese traders used the Silk Road to export luxury goods such as lacquerware, porcelain, tea, and spices to Europe and Asia. On their way back to China, the traders also brought goods such as grape wine, figs, and Islamic and Byzantine glassware.

During the 3–4th century BC, the silks of the kingdom of Qin reached northern India. The Indians named China after the Qin dynasty (pronounced "chin"), so we got the name "China" via India. The Romans, who loved Chinese silk, which was carried on the backs of camels and horses from the Chinese capital Chang'an thousands of miles westwards to Europe, referred to China as "Seres" or "the land of silk." The Chinese kept silk production methods a secret up until the 5th century. Before then, people in the West believed that silk came from plants! Since they didn't know how it was made, they could only buy it from China.

The painting above shows silk being made. Silk is actually made from the unbroken cocoons of silk worms (see picture top left).

The first Buddhist monks came to China in the 1st century AD. This monk is shown carrying Buddhist scrolls.

China and the World

Luxury goods such as teas, spices, and items made from jade and porcelain were also carried along the Silk Road. These were highly prized in Asia and Europe. However, the Silk Road did not only exchange goods. Some of the world's greatest inventions came from China, such as the magnetic compass, fireworks, kites, umbrellas, and paper and printing. Many of these ideas were carried along the Silk Road into Europe and Asia.

Bactrian (two-humped) camels were the main means of transport along the Silk Road.

Life on the Road

Chinese merchants traveled in groups, called caravans, as protection against raiders from the north. After the merchants had passed the last outpost of the empire in northern China, called the Jade Gates, they had to rely on the occasional oasis to buy supplies for themselves and their animals. It was a perilous journey. In the Gobi Desert, for example, temperatures during the day reached 113°F and fell to as low as -40°F at night.

The three-colored (sancai) ceramic plate shown here imitated the design of Islamic glassware. Many foreign influences were brought to China along the Silk Road.

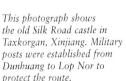

This photograph shows the old Silk Road castle in Taxkorgan, Xinjiang. Military posts were established from Dunhuang to Lop Nor to protect the route.

FOOD AND MEDICINE

Chinese food was prepared in a number of different ways – stir-fried, steamed, or simmered with spices such as star aniseed, sesame oils, and soy sauce. Some foods were regarded as medicinal and attributed with powers that affected the health of the body.

The Chinese have al[so] enjoyed adding herbs [and] spices to food. Cinnamon[,] ginger, pictured above, [are] popular flavor[s.]

The staple food of most Chinese in the north was millet, while the southern Chinese ate rice. People ate simple foods, such as vegetables and beans, and very little meat. At banquets, rich people enjoyed foods like minced fish, quails, oranges, and pickles.

Noodles

Large-scale flour grinding became widespread during the Han dynasty (207 BC–AD 220) when the flour mill was introduced. People used the flour mill to produce a great variety of new

Many Chinese herbs, as shown on the left, were first dried in the sun. Angelica, on the right, was used as a medicine as well as for cooking.

These tasty flou[r] pastries were typica[l] delicacies of th[e] Tang perio[d] (AD 618–906)[.]

dishes such as noodles, steamed buns, and baked cakes similar to those shown above. By the first century AD, noodle stands were doing a good business in the city marketplaces. By the second century, even the emperor ate them.

This Han dynasty drinking vessel is called an "ear cup." It was held carefully with both hands and the wine it contained drunk during banquets.

Yin and Yang

According to Chinese philosophy, there were two opposing forces in nature called the yin and the yang, which existed in a delicate state of balance. The Chinese believed that a healthy diet was the correct balancing of the yin and yang of food. Ingredients were either yin (cold) or yang (hot). In winter, one would eat yang foods, such as chickens stewed with ginseng (an aromatic root) which warmed up the body. Melon soup was a remedy for sore throats because its yin was believed to counteract inflammations suffered by the patient.

In this painting, a boy is being told about the yin and yang which is shown by the circular sign on the scroll.

Life Forces

The Chinese had many theories about the human body. Doctors prescribed a variety of herbal medicines to treat illnesses. For example, Chinese yam was used to treat fatigue and loss of appetite. Acupuncture was based on the theory that the life force of the body flowed along 12 lines, or meridians. Each meridian was linked to a different organ. Doctors inserted small needles, first sterilized in fire, into certain points of the body to relieve pain or treat illnesses, including arthritis and stomach ulcers.

This chart shows some of the 650 needle points of the body.

CLOTHES AND JEWELRY

A person's status in ancient China was reflected by their clothes. The poor dressed in rough, hard-wearing materials, while the rich wore fine silk robes. Jewelry was worn for decoration and also as a sign of rank.

Peasants wore sandals and wide brim hats made from woven, dried grass to ward off sun stroke and rain. Humble people in cities wore scarves wrapped around their hair. Laborers wore loose clothes made of hemp, a rough material made from plant fibers. Women wore long tunics, belted or tied at the waist, and short jackets.

From ancient times, belt hooks, plaques, and buckles were important accessories for men.

This shoe is made from hard-wearing material, such as hemp, and probably belonged to a laborer.

Clothes for the Rich

To ward off the cold, rich city folk wore woolen robes lined with ferret fur, while nobles wore the furs of squirrels and foxes, or wild duck plumes. Silk, though, was always the material of prestige. Noble women wore beautiful silk robes, richly embroidered with delicate flowers. Scholar officials had elaborate hats made of stiff cloth secured by strings that attached beneath the chin. Silk-cloth bands, called *shou*, indicated rank by length. The more noble the official's position, the longer the *shou* – the

Porcelain figure of a Taoist deity wearing the robes of a scholar official.

In your tray there is a Chinese fan to decorate with the stickers in your drawer. Fans were usually made of paper and wood, and decorated with elaborate designs.

emperor, of course, had the longest *shou* of all. Some officials wore their *shou* tied in front of their stomachs, allowing it to drape down towards the floor. Others preferred to keep it in a little pouch on their belt, along with their official seal.

Makeup and Jewelry

A rich or titled man might wear buckles made of gold and silver. These were sometimes carved with leopards or mythical beasts. Women piled their hair high into intricate shapes and decorated it with up to ten hairpins made of gold and silver and precious stones.

During the Tang dynasty (AD 618–906), women sprinkled their foreheads with gold dust, and stuck vermilion or green paper designs on them as beauty marks. Fans were also a favorite accessory for both men and women. Educated men enjoyed

This beautiful comb may have belonged to a noble woman. Women also wore gold and silver jewelry in their hair.

writing a favorite poem on their fans, while women's fans were usually decorated with flowers and trees.

Chinese women favored elaborate hairstyles, held in place by hairpins. As the women walked, the hairpins made delightful clinks, considered one of the feminine charms.

ENTERTAINMENT AND GAMES

The Chinese spent much of their precious spare time playing dice, cards, and other gambling games. The Chinese calendar also included several national festivals, the most important of which was New Year, when family members exchanged gifts and shared a large feast.

There is a Chinese calendar disk in your drawer.

Acrobats and sword jugglers performed at funerals, weddings, births, and any other events with large crowds – even at beheadings. Country peasants came to markets to see puppeteers, dancers, musical entertainers, and performing animals, such as bears. City people might take their children to parks to go rowing on the lakes. During festivals, kites were flown. The Chinese invented kites 3,000 years ago.

The Chinese believed that music was an essential part of life. Models of musicians were often placed in tombs to entertain the dead in the afterlife.

Entertainment for the Rich

The rich enjoyed listening to music with orchestras of bells, flutes, drums, and the *qin* (a seven-stringed instrument that was plucked). Educated people played word games and riddles, and sharp-tongued jesters were sometimes as highly valued as

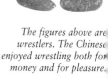

The figures above are wrestlers. The Chinese enjoyed wrestling both for money and for pleasure.

The painting above shows a child capturing a grasshopper. Children in the countryside often made pets of insects and small birds.

officials in imperial courts. Nobles also enjoyed active sports, such as archery or horse-riding. Emperor Chen of the Han liked to play kickball with the court ladies, while Tang nobles enjoyed playing polo, a game that originated in Persia.

Games of Strategy

Go, a popular board game, was first invented by the Emperor Yao for his son Dan Zhu, who liked to pick fights and to gamble. Games such as Go and Chinese chess were popular with military tacticians and literary men alike.

Dancers and acrobats, shown here as clay figures, were popular forms of entertainment.

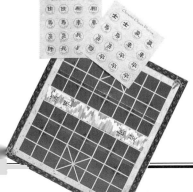

Inside your secret drawer there is a board and pieces that you can use to play Chinese chess. The pieces include cavalry, chariots, a general, and artillery.

LEARNING AND SCHOLARSHIP

Most children in ancient China did not recieve a formal education. They either stayed on the farms or learned a trade or craft. Only rich families could afford to educate their children in reading and writing, which would lead them to careers in the civil service.

This painting shows children reading and writing. Wealthy families often had their own schools and cousins would study together.

In poor families, girls started working at an early age. Their duties included taking care of younger brothers and sisters, cooking, cleaning, and running a household. Boys helped their fathers on the farms. Sometimes, families would pool their resources and ask a failed metropolitan examination candidate – a *xiu cai* (a candidate who passed provincial examinations) – to teach promising young village boys in exchange for room, board, and a small salary.

Trades and Crafts in the Cities

In the cities, children were apprenticed to tofu makers, carpenters, or blacksmiths from as young as 12 years of age. They were usually apprenticed to their own fathers or to tradesmen known to their parents. Often, secret skills or recipes would be handed down from one generation to the next, from father to son,

Lacquerwork was an important Chinese craft. This lacquer stag dates from 5th century BC.

Chinese writing consists of more than 40,000 symbols. Each one is a small picture and the writing is read from right to left.

or mother to daughter. That is why some trademarks, even today, bear a family name such as Kong Family Fine Wine, or Wu's Soft Tofu.

Private Education

Rich families relied upon private tutors and their own libraries to educate their sons in hopes of glory at the examinations. Teachers, like Confucius, often attracted students to their schools from all parts of China.

State Education

Public colleges existed from as early as 124 BC. These were mainly for noble children. Pupils were given an examination at the age of 18 or 20 and, according to their scores, they were placed in the civil service. Gradually, these exams became available to everyone.

The first Chinese writing evolved during the Shang period, when priest-kings communicated with their ancestors by carving questions on oracle bones like the one on the right.

WARFARE

Throughout its long history, China was often at war and a variety of weapons were invented. During the Warring States period, a military tactician named Sunzi wrote Art of War, *the world's oldest military handbook.*

Chariots were introduced from the West during the Shang dynasty (*c.* 1650–1027 BC). However, they became less important after the crossbow was invented around 450 BC. Crossbow archers could bring down the charioteers from a safe distance. During the Warring States period (403–221 BC), large-scale battles took place between cavalry, chariots, and crossbowmen. Thousands were killed. Some kingdoms, such as Yan (present-day Beijing) became major producers of iron, which was tougher than bronze. Iron knives, axes, and helmets provided soldiers with better protection and more deadly weaponry.

There is a model of a Great Wall watchtower in your secret drawer to assemble.

The Great Wall

By the 4th century BC, northern peoples began raiding China. The late Zhou states on the northern frontier started to build defensive walls as protection. During the Qin dynasty (221–207 BC) these walls were joined into one, long Great Wall. Under the Han, the wall

This figure of a foot soldier dates from the Han dynasty (207 BC–AD 220). His armor was made of leather plates sewn together, and a neck protector.

was extended from the Eastern Sea to the fort of Dunhuang near the Gobi Desert. Stretching nearly 6,500 miles, it is the longest structure ever built. The Wall originally had some 25,000 defensive watchtowers. Arrows, water jars, braziers for cooking, and medicine chests were kept locked inside the towers.

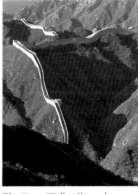

The Great Wall still stands across northern China today.

Each watchtower had one squad of soldiers. Any movements in the north were quickly reported using signal flags by day and beacon fires by night.

Kung Fu

Chinese martial arts are a combination of Indian and Chinese combat skills. Individual warriors practiced *wu gong* (kung fu), which was started by a 7th-century Indian monk, called Bodhidarma. He settled in central China, in the Shaolin temple, where he faced a cave wall for nine years. On reaching enlightenment, he began teaching the fundamentals of martial arts.

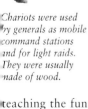

Chariots were used by generals as mobile command stations and for light raids. They were usually made of wood.

Bodhidarma taught the Shaolin Style of combat, which emphasized solid kicking and punching methods, as well as controled breathing.

ARCHAEOLOGY

Although some of ancient China's past was excavated during the early part of the 20th century, much of it still lies buried underground.

This silk banner shows the Buddha preaching. It was found in the Dunhuang caves.

In the 1930s, the Swedish geologist J.G. Anderson excavated the site of Zhoukoudian, north of Beijing. It is the richest site in China for Neolithic (late Stone Age) fossils. During the early part of the century, archaeologists Sir Marc Aurel Stein and Paul Pelliot brought back hundreds of silk and paper scrolls from the Buddhist caves of Dunhuang.

The First Emperor was buried along with an army of terra cotta soldiers and life-size horses and chariots.

The Terra Cotta Army

In 1975, farmers digging a well found the body of a life-size clay soldier. When Chinese archaeologists dug in the area, they found an enormous pit, containing 6,000 infantrymen, life-size in unfired clay, also known as terra cotta.

The Jade Shroud

Early in 1996, Chinese archaeologists digging in eastern China unearthed the tomb of Liu Wu, a ruler of the Han dynasty. Hundreds of relics in gold, silver, and bronze have been found as well as Liu Wu's jade shroud, in which he was buried around 174 BC. The exquisite shroud consists of 4,000 wafer-thin plaques of jade, sewn together with gold thread.

An empty tomb chamber of the Han period.